GOODNIGHT COWTOWN

Written by
Jennifer Gaines Drez &
Robin Beal Bumstead

Illustrated by
Lisa Carrington Voight

Published by Petit Chou Chou, LLC
PO Box 470875
Fort Worth, Texas 76147

First Printing
ISBN-13: 978-0-615-54492-2 / ISBN-10: 0-615-54492-4
Printed in Canada

To order additional copies of this book, please visit:
www.goodnightcowtown.com

For Bass, David, Merrill, Phillip, Patrick, Jud, Mary Evans, Sawyer, and Witt.
We love you.

The sun is setting on the city of culture and the cowboy.

It's time to say goodnight to all that we enjoy.

Goodnight Camp Bowie with your red bricks.

Goodnight Kincaid's, Angelo's,
and other favorite picks.

Goodnight Trinity River.
Goodnight trails.

Goodnight runners, cyclers,
and dogs with wagging tails.

Goodnight to
the Kimbell,
the Carter,
and the Modern.

Goodnight to the Symphony
and Concerts in the Garden.

Goodnight dinosaurs.
Goodnight cowgirls.

Goodnight to the Ballet and dancers who twirl.

Goodnight to the Library and buildings so tall.

Goodnight Sundance Square.

Goodnight Bass Hall.

Goodnight Van Cliburn.
Goodnight Opera.

Goodnight to the children performing at Casa.

Goodnight
rodeo clowns.

Goodnight
Stock Show.

Goodnight Midway, funnel cakes, and nachos.

Goodnight to saddles
and boots made by hand.

Goodnight Joe T's and the mariachi band.

Goodnight Billy Bob's and music that's live.

Goodnight two-stepping.

Goodnight
cattle drive.

Goodnight animals at the Fort Worth Zoo.

Goodnight MOLA and the zoo train, too.

Goodnight golfers
on the Colonial greens.

Goodnight to the Horned Frogs, our home team!

Goodnight to the Rangers
and fans celebrating big wins!

Goodnight
Fort Worth...

Acknowledgements

This book only touches on Fort Worth's rich heritage and culture.
We hope adults and children alike will be inspired by the images and words
in this book and experience a deeper, more meaningful connection with the city
of cowboys and culture.

We appreciate the support of the establishments mentioned in
Goodnight Cowtown
and hope they live on in the minds and hearts of this generation
and many more to come.

Why is Fort Worth called "Cowtown"?

In the late 1800s, Fort Worth, named for Major General William Jenkins Worth
(1794-1849), was the last major stop for rest and supplies before heading cattle up
the Chisholm Trail. Beyond Fort Worth, where the West truly began, the ranchers
would have to cross rough terrain, including Indian Territory. More than four
million head of cattle were brought through Fort Worth between 1866 and 1890,
giving it the nickname "Cowtown."

Camp Bowie Boulevard

In 1917, Camp Bowie, a World War I training center named for Captain Jim Bowie, was home to the U.S. Army's 36th Infantry Division. The Boulevard serves as a tribute to the Fort Worth-trained soldiers who fought and died in World War I. In the late 1920s, the Boulevard was paved with thousands of red bricks, and portions are still bricked today.

Kincaid's Hamburgers

Charles Kincaid's Grocery and Market was established September 5, 1946, in Fort Worth, Texas. In 1964, O.R. Gentry, the store butcher since 1947, began cooking his famous hamburgers, drawing crowds from all over Tarrant County. Gentry purchased Kincaid's in 1967, and it is still family owned and operated today.

Angelo's Barbeque

Angelo's Barbeque is family owned and operated and has been a Fort Worth favorite since its opening in 1958. Angelo's casual atmosphere is enhanced by the abundant display of hunting trophies. The establishment is filled with the wonderful aroma of hickory smoked beef and is considered among the country's best barbeque.

Trinity River and the Trinity River Trails

The Trinity River provides over 40 miles of trails for walking, running, and cycling. This network of trails connects many of the city's parks and attractions and has been home to MayFest, one of Fort Worth's most popular family festivals, since 1973.

Kimbell Art Museum

The Kimbell Art Museum, designed by Louis I. Kahn (1901-1974), is known as one of the most outstanding architectural achievements of our time. The design of the building enhances the experience and highlights the artwork within. The Kimbell's permanent collection includes important and quality pieces spanning from antiquity to the 20th century.

Amon Carter Museum of American Art

The Amon Carter Museum of American Art houses a preeminent collection of nineteenth and twentieth-century painting, sculpture, and works on paper. It is also one of the nation's major repositories of American photography. Admission to the permanent collection, special exhibitions, and enriching public programs for all ages is always free.

Modern Art Museum of Fort Worth

Dedicated to "collecting, presenting, and interpreting international developments in post-World War II art in all media," the Modern Art Museum of Fort Worth showcases a renowned collection of modern and contemporary art from around the world. The building, designed by Japanese architect Tadao Ando, features fifty-three thousand square feet of gallery space and casts breath-taking reflections in a one and one-half acre pond.

Fort Worth Symphony Orchestra

The Fort Worth Symphony Orchestra, the primary resident of the acoustically superb Bass Performance Hall, was founded in 1912. The FWSO has a 46-week season presenting a series of symphonic, pops, and special concerts. It also serves as the orchestra for the Fort Worth Opera, the Van Cliburn International Piano Competition, and various local choruses.

Fort Worth Botanic Garden

The Fort Worth Botanic Garden was established in 1934 and is the oldest botanic garden in Texas. The Botanic Garden is well-known for its 23 specialty gardens, the annual "Concerts in the Garden" series, and for the fall and spring festivals in the Japanese Gardens. The Botanic Garden "enriches peoples' lives through environmental stewardship and education."

Fort Worth Museum of Science and History

From its humble beginnings in an elementary school in 1941 to its current 166,000 square-foot facility designed by the internationally acclaimed architect, Legoretta + Legoretta, the Fort Worth Museum of Science and History has been dedicated to providing "an extraordinary learning environment to the community." The Museum welcomes around 1 million guests each year and hosts educational exhibits such as The DinoLabs and DinoDig, The Cattle Raisers Museum, The Fort Worth Children's Museum, and Energy Blast.

National Cowgirl Museum and Hall of Fame

The National Cowgirl Museum and Hall of Fame is the only museum in the world dedicated to honoring women of the American West who have displayed extraordinary courage and pioneering fortitude. Since it was established in 1975, the Museum has become an invaluable educational resource nationally known for its exhibits, artifacts, research library, rare photography collection, and the 200+ honorees in its Hall of Fame.

Texas Ballet Theater

Founded in 1961 by Margo Dean, Texas Ballet Theater has grown from a small civic dance company into the second largest professional ballet company in Texas. Formally known as the Fort Worth Ballet, TBT brings unprecedented talent, beauty, and artistic expression as the resident ballet company for Bass Performance Hall.

Fort Worth Public Library

The city's first library, which opened in 1901, was the idea of 20 local women and funded by wealthy philanthropist, Andrew Carnegie. The public library system has grown with Fort Worth and provides important programming in literacy, education, and access to literature for children and adults of all ages.

Sundance Square

Located downtown, Sundance Square hosts dynamic festivals, concerts, charity walks, and more. Sundance Square is home to a multitude of restaurants, galleries, shops, and museums.

Nancy Lee and Perry R. Bass Performance Hall

Characteristic of the classic European opera house, the Nancy Lee and Perry R. Bass Performance Hall is the crown jewel of Fort Worth. The Hall's two 48-foot tall angels that grace the façade have become cultural icons of the Fort Worth community. The Bass Hall is home to Fort Worth Symphony Orchestra, Texas Ballet Theater, Fort Worth Opera, Van Cliburn International Piano Competition, and Cliburn Concerts.

Van Cliburn

In 1958, Fort Worth's Van Cliburn achieved worldwide recognition at the age of 23, when he won the first International Tchaikovsky Piano Competition in Moscow at the height of the Cold War. Since 1962, the Van Cliburn Foundation has held a quadrennial international piano competition in Fort Worth. The Foundation's mission is "to showcase extraordinary talent and promote excellence in classical music worldwide through piano competitions, concerts, and educational programs."

Fort Worth Opera

The Fort Worth Opera, dating back to 1946, is one of the 14 oldest opera companies in the nation. The Opera offers a four week condensed performance schedule every Spring and is also known for its excellent educational programs presented to school-aged children across the state of Texas.

Casa Manana

Casa Manana, "The Theatre of Tomorrow," which was created in 1957, has grown into the largest performing arts organization in Tarrant County. Programming includes Broadway musicals, the Children's Playhouse, and Casa Manana's Theatre School. In 2003, Casa was renovated into a state of the art performance venue that attracts over 150,000 people annually.

Fort Worth Stock Show and Rodeo

The Fort Worth Stock Show and Rodeo was established in 1896. The Stock Show is a highly anticipated annual event. Packed with tradition and courageous cowboys, it is a wonderful educational opportunity for all. The event includes a premier livestock and horse show, live music, a carnival midway, and shopping.

Will Rogers Coliseum and Memorial Center

The Will Rogers Coliseum and landmark Pioneer Tower were erected in 1936, the year of the Texas Centennial. The Coliseum was the first domed structure of its kind in the world. Will Rogers is spread over 85 acres in the heart of the Fort Worth Cultural District. It is a multi-purpose entertainment complex best known for hosting the Fort Worth Stock Show and Rodeo.

M. L. Leddy's

Since 1922, M.L. Leddy's has been providing its customers with handmade boots and saddles. A second location was opened in the Fort Worth Stockyards in 1941. Still family owned, the fourth generation continues the tradition of quality and customer service that began almost 90 years ago.

Joe T Garcia's

Mr. and Mrs. Joe T. Garcia established their namesake restaurant July 4, 1935, with seating for sixteen people. Thanks to its mouth-watering recipes and beautiful patio area, the family owned and operated restaurant has grown to a seating capacity of well over a thousand people. The famous enchiladas and fajitas are a delight to both locals and tourists.

Billy Bob's Texas

"The World's Largest Honkytonk" has become a legend in live music by hosting virtually every major country artist since its opening in 1981. Located in the Fort Worth Stockyards, Billy Bob's has its own restaurant and indoor rodeo arena with competitive bull riding every weekend.

Fort Worth Stockyards National Historic District

The Fort Worth Stockyards is an important part of Fort Worth history and the history of the livestock industry in Texas. The Stockyards also hosts the world's only twice daily cattle drive.

Fort Worth Zoo

The nationally acclaimed Fort Worth Zoo is home to more than 500 animal species, as well as a world-famous reptile collection housed in the award-winning Museum of Living Art (MOLA). The Zoo's focus on education and conservation is second to none, enhancing the lives of more than 1 million visitors a year.

Colonial National Invitation Tournament

Founded in 1946, Colonial is the longest-running PGA Tour event being held at its original site. Five-time winner and hometown legend Ben Hogan helped bring notoriety and exposure to Fort Worth through the tournament, which raises millions of dollars each year for area charities. The Colonial golf course is consistently rated in the country's top 100 courses, and the tournament is among the most prestigious in championship golf around the world.

Texas Christian University

Texas Christian University, located in the heart of Fort Worth, was founded in 1873 and offers both undergraduate and graduate areas of study. The TCU Horned Frogs have brought home two national football championships and are cheered on by students, alumni, and Fort Worth residents alike.

Texas Rangers

Originally franchised in 1961, the Arlington-based Texas Rangers are members of Major League Baseball's American League. Fort Worth fans have enjoyed cheering them on to five division titles and two league championships.

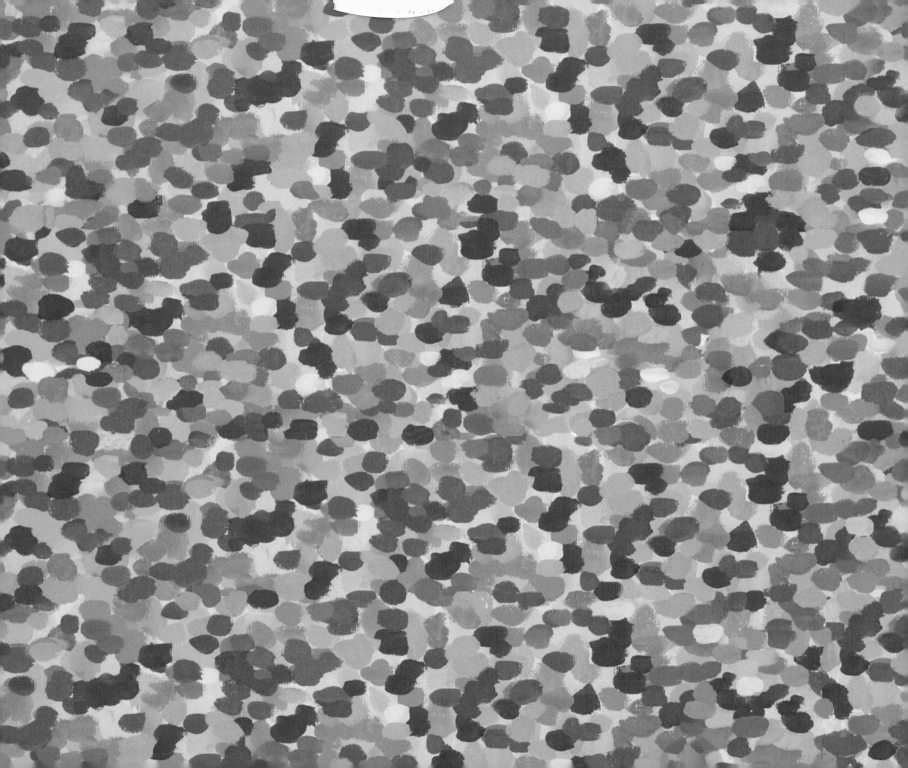